BEDSIDE MANNER

Dedicated to the
Medical Profession
with sincere thanks.

Especially for:

_____

Special thanks and appreciation to

Dr. Dobkin,
Dr. Hagler,
Dr. Walsh,
Carol Pawlaski, RN
and
Claire Gavigan, RN
for being there for Amy.

Cover design by: Jeff Maniglia
Compiled by: Peggy Schaffer

Copyright © 1991, Great Quotations, Inc.

All rights reserved. No part of this publication may be reproduced, stored in a retrieval system, or transmitted in any form by any means, electronic, mechanical, photocopying, recording or otherwise without the prior consent of Great Quotations, Inc.

ISBN: 1-56245-052-2

An ounce of prevention is worth a pound of cure.

Other Great Quotations Books:

- The Book of Proverbs
- Aged to Perfection
- Retirement
- Love on Your Wedding Day
- Thinking of You
- The Unofficial Executive Survival Guide
- Inspirations
- Sports Poop
- Over the Hill
- Golf Humor
- Happy Birthday to the Golfer
- Stress
- Cat Tales
- The Unofficial Christmas Survival Guide
- The Unofficial Survival Guide To Parenthood
- A Smile Increases Your Face Value
- Keys to Happiness
- Things You'll Learn...
- Teachers Inspirations
- Boyfriends Live Longer than...
- Worms of Wisdom
- Our Life Together
- Thoughts from the Hear
- An Apple a Day
- The Joy of Family
- What to Tell Your Children
- Proverbs Vol. II
- A Friend is a Present
- Books are Better in Bed then Men

GREAT QUOTATIONS, INC.
1967 Quincy Ct. • Glendale Heights, IL 60139

TOLL FREE: 800-354-4889 (outside Illinois)
(708) 582-2800
PRINTED IN HONG KONG

Medicine may be the only profession that labors incessantly to destroy the reason for its own existence.

Hospitals stifle individuality ... Everyone dresses the same.

A patient in the hands of a doctor is like a hero in the hands of a good writer. He's going to suffer a great deal, but he's going to come out all right in the end.

— Finley Peter Dunne

Happiness? That's nothing more than health and a poor memory.

— Albert Schweitzer

Show him death and he'll be content with fever.

— Persian Proverb

All diseases run into one, old age.

— Emerson

I enjoyed convalescence. It is the part that makes illness worth while.

— George Bernard Shaw

Study sickness while you are well.

— Thomas Fuller

Patience is the best medicine.

— John Florio

The test of the medical profession is the love of the drudgery it involves.

The first wealth is health.

— Emerson

It does your ulcers absolutely no good to wonder how many of your doctor's kids you've put through college.

Remember while you
are in the hospital;
there are three kinds of lies:

lies,
damned lies,
and
statistics
!

After the verb "To Love", "To Help" is the most beautiful verb in the world.

— Bertha von Sutter

Whatever happens, do not lose hold of the two main ropes of life — hope and faith.

The best doctor in the world is a Veterinarian. He can't ask his patients what is the matter - he's got to just know.

— Will Rogers

God heals, and the doctor takes the fees.

— Benjamin Franklin

We have not lost faith, but we have transferred it to the medical profession.

— George Bernard Shaw

My doctor is nice; every time I see him I'm ashamed of what I think of doctors in general.

— Mignon Mclaughlin

The test of how sick you are is whether you can joke about it.

Mary had a little Lamb.
The doctor fainted.

You know you are staying in a deluxe hospital when you have your own remote control . . . and it's for the bedpan!

Asthma is a disease that has practically the same symptoms as passion, except that with asthma it lasts longer.

We've made great medical progress in the last generation. What used to be merely an itch is now an allergy.

Nature, time, and patience are the three great cures.

You may not be able to read a doctor's handwriting and prescription, but, you'll notice his bills are neatly typewritten.

— Earl Wilson

If you consider what doctors charge, the most precious stones are not diamonds and emeralds - they're gall and kidney.

— Robert Oren

Every man has his own vocation. The talent is the call.

— Emerson

Every calling is great when greatly pursued.

— Oliver Wendell Holmes

Keep watch also on the faults of the patients, which often make them lie about taking of things prescribed.

— Hippocrates

All interest in disease and death is only another expression of interest in life.

— Thomas Mann

It is medicine, not scenery, for which a sick man must go searching.

— Seneca

Experience is not what happens to a man, it is what a man does with what happens to him.

— Aldous Huxley

I got the bill for my surgery. Now I know why those doctors were wearing masks.

— James H. Barrie

A rule of thumb in the matter of medical advice is to take everything any doctor says with a grain of aspirin.

— Goodman Ace

A hospital should also have a recovery room adjoining the cashier's office.

— Francis O'Walsh

The pen is mightier than the sword! The case for prescription rather than surgery.

— Marvin Kitman

You can only cure retail, but, you can prevent wholesale.

— Brock Chisholm

Laughter is a tranquilizer with no side effects.

— Arnold Glasow

The art of medicine consists of amusing the patient while nature cures the disease.

— Voltaire

I don't see why any man who believes in medicine would shy at the faith cure.

— Finley Peter Dunne

She got her good looks from her father — he's a plastic surgeon.

— Groucho Marx

There was a day when an apple a day kept the doctor away, but now it's malpractice insurance.

— Laurence J. Peter

A vasectomy is never having to say you're sorry.

— Rubin Carson

A nurse always checks the patients' pulses, and sometimes their impulses.

After two days in the hospital, I took a turn for the nurse.

— W. C. Fields

Nobody ever died of laughter.

— Max Beerbohm

A psychiatrist is a fellow who asks you a lot of expensive questions your wife asks for nothing.

— Joey Adams

The world is divided into two classes — invalids and nurses.

— James McNeill Whistler

One group of doctors who still make housecalls: coroners.

— Malcolm Forbes

Middle age is when a man is warned to slow down by his doctor instead of a policeman.

A neurotic is
the man who builds a
castle in the air.
A psychotic is
the man who lives in it.
A psychiatrist is
the man who
collects the rent.

An ailing woman lives forever.

— Spanish Proverb

Sickness is felt, but health not at all.

— Thomas Fuller

Laughter is the sensation of feeling good allover and showing it principally in one place.

— Josh Billings

Psychiatrist — a person who pulls habits out of rats.

— Dr. Douglas Bush

In spite of the cost of living it's still popular.

— Kathleen Norris

**If I had known
I was going to
live this long
I would have taken
better care
of myself.**

I don't jog. If I die, I want to be sick.

— Abe Lemons

Wherever the art of medicine is loved, there also is love of humanity.

— Hippocrates

There are no such
things as incurables;
there are only things
for which man
has not found a cure.

— Bernard M. Baruch

We are healthy only to the extent that our ideas are humane.

— Kurt Vonnegut, Jr.

Scientific and humanist approaches are not competitive but supportive, and both are ultimately necessary.

— Robert C. Wood

What can be added to the happiness of a man who is in health, out of debt, and has a clear conscience?

— Adam Smith

I'm not afraid to die. I just don't want to be there when it happens.

— Woody Allen

Everyone in my family follows the medical profession. They're all lawyers.

Only a fool would make a doctor his heir.

— Russian Proverb

There are worse occupations in this world than feeling a woman's pulse.

— Laurence Sterne

It is amazing that a doctor can put a tongue depressor in your mouth and open your wallet at the same time.

Doctors may have all the patients, but it's the nurse that calls all the shots!

— Laura Mauk

Hospitals merely replace "physical pain" with "financial drain".

There are two things a hospital will leave you without:

MONEY
&
DIGNITY

It's bad news when your doctor tells you that if you were a horse they would have shot you by now.

More people rust than wear out.

The best news you'll ever hear from your doctor is: "No news is good news!"

— Bonnie Domingo

Hygiene is the corruption of medicine by morality.

— H. L. Mencken